Cafeteria Covenant

The Voice, The Choice, and The Challenge

All Scripture from *The Voice* unless otherwise noted
Cover design by Dee Marvin Emeigh

ISBN-13:
978-0615633756
Livingwell Press

ISBN-10:
0615633757

Contents

Author's Note

Throughout this book, you will find the term "church" applied in three distinctly different ways:

1. Church (upper case C):
The universal, corporate, and eternal body of all Christian believers, across denominations and time. This includes those who are members of this body even though they are no longer alive on the earth.

2. church (lower case c):
The gathering of local Christian believers, usually within a specified building on a weekly basis for a service of worship; also, the service of worship that takes place in such a building.

3. *church* (lower case italics):
That which comprises the general body of all Christian believers *presently alive* on earth, regardless of denomination.

Preface

A page from my notebook

November 1, 2010 - David's 'last will and testament,' found in 2 Samuel 23:5

"Yes, God has made an everlasting covenant with me. His agreement is eternal, final, sealed. He will constantly look after my safety and success" (TLB).

Despite his trials, David never lost faith in God. The same, everlasting covenant David had with God is available to everyone who enters into it. I am not sure I ever thought about it that way.

Many people talk about being saved and accepting Jesus, making him Lord. Yet, I have yet to hear anyone say, 'I have entered into a covenant with God' (or with Jesus).

This covenant provides us with 'all things pertaining to life and godliness,' but we make the choices. God has already done His part. He has kept His covenant, and we can enter into it by choice and choose to believe what we will.

I choose to abide in the covenant of an incredible, living God, and I will gladly feast on all that he has given his life to give me...

–

And so it began... a gradual understanding of the covenant that provides "all things pertaining to life and godliness,"[1] to those who receive it measure by measure. In this sense it is like a cafeteria, a place full of choices, where we can take what we will, but all of it is ours by faith.

In this, the 12th anniversary edition of *Cafeteria Covenant,* I have refined the message, using a more powerful, and perhaps more pure lens, to share what I now more clearly and confidently assert as a vital message for the church of Jesus Christ. I have come to realize that the waypoints on my journey served as a virtual cafeteria that together resulted in a deeper understanding of our covenant with the Almighty.

A year after I wrote the original journal entry, I began to sense the need to chronicle my journey. I now understand that in part, this

---

1   2 Peter 1:3

chronicle is so that you and I may meet somewhere along that road of shared experience.

For many years, I had known in my spirit that God would have me write a book. He had said so, but I had not known where to start or what I was supposed to write about. I had kept journals for years, but which of the revelatory experiences did God want me to share?

As I sought Him, He began to reveal the following objectives as a framework for all that would be written in this book; that is, those things this book would serve to impart:

Wisdom – to impart the ability to extract the precious from the worthless[2]

Knowledge – to give assurance of hearing His Voice and trusting His leading.

Discipleship – to teach about working out our faith in due diligence[3] instead of settling or

---

2"Therefore, thus says the LORD, 'If you return, then I will restore you-- Before Me you will stand; And if you extract the precious from the worthless, You will become My spokesman. They for their part may turn to you, But as for you, you must not turn to them'" (Jeremiah 15:19, New American Standard Version).

3   "So now, my beloved, obey as you have always done, not only when I am with you, but even more so when I can't be. Continue to work out your salvation, with great fear and trembling" (Philippians 2:12).

compromising for a form of godliness that denies His power[4]

Admonition – to accept responsibility for (the power of) the words we speak.

Encouragement – to recognize and experience God's presence outside the walls of the church.

Community – to see the importance of fellowship with the saints from all the ages and all the expressions of His body[5]

Living Sacrifice[6] - to offer myself as a vessel in answer to the prayer of Jesus, Himself, on the night he was betrayed:

"May they be one even as We are one."

John 17:11

---

4 II Timothy 3:1-5
5 Alicia Britt Chole, *The Making of a Mentor,* 2001
6 Romans 12:1

Introduction

When this book was first released in 2011, it was the testimony of a long journey — five decades of following the Shepherd's voice, seeking God's design for the church Jesus set out to establish. Twelve years later, the message has only deepened. The world has changed. The church has shifted. But the covenant of Christ remains the same. This edition has been refined — names removed, details sharpened, insights clarified — so that the focus remains not on me, but on the One who calls His people back to His table.

For most of forty years, I was a *participating visitor* in local churches. This description is derived from the prophetic word of a man whose name I have long ago forgotten, but whose word resonated again and again across those years. The implication was that I would be an active part of many different churches, not merely as a passive pew sitter, but as an integral part of the ministry. I didn't really understand why this would be, because it was contrary to anyone's concept of the proper way to serve God, even my own; that is, to "grow where you are planted." Yet, in spite of a good deal of resistance on my part, it proved true.

Part One tells the backstory, the qualifications for the message delivered in the second part. So as not to give offense, I have changed names and removed some details from the first printing. This refining of purpose is also meant to deter the reader from thinking this is just a story about me. Moreover, as stated in the preface, it is written so that you, the reader, might gain an understanding of the process of God's working and refining, as well as identifying with His purpose for us in this world.

As a disclaimer, I humbly add the following words from the Apostle Paul for your consideration:

> *I did not pose as an expert with all the answers. I did not pretend to explain the mystery of God with eloquent speech and human wisdom. I claimed to know nothing with certainty other than the reality that Jesus is the Anointed One, the Liberating King, who was crucified on our behalf....The sermons I preached were not delivered with the kind of persuasive elegance some have come to expect, but they were effective because I relied on God's Spirit to demonstrate*

God's power. If this were not so, your faith would be based on human wisdom and not the power of God (1 Corinthians 2:1–5).

Regardless of Paul's years of education, his training for what God called him to do came directly from the Holy Spirit of God. Only God can prepare men and women for the work He is calling them to do, and He chooses the coaches and trainers.

When Saul met Jesus through His Holy Spirit, his life became drastically different. The new convert, who was given a new name, Paul, was not sent to Jerusalem to be taught by those who had known Jesus in the flesh. Instead, the Holy Spirit led him to Arabia, to unlearn all the old ways and learn the new ones. He spent three years there, learning directly from the Holy Spirit.

This process of learning and unlearning, of separating the precious from the worthless, is vital to the life of Christ in us, and therefore, in the world. In fact, it can be a matter of life and death. Consider the following example:

As I was preparing to leave for a meeting one morning, I noticed a Facebook post from a popular women's ministry: "The devil has no power but that which you give him." I was pondering this as I approached the intersection of the highway in my little Honda Civic an hour later. Not exactly true, I mused. The whole world is under the devil's power, and people (even those who are closest to us) are used every day to accomplish his work.

I waited to cross the four-lane divided highway, noting a large white Cadillac SUV waiting in the median. No turn signal indicated that the SUV was going to turn across my lane, so I assumed the driver was proceeding straight. I began to move across the two open lanes of traffic and the SUV turned into my path, accelerating so fast that I was directly positioned for a serious accident.

I honked and honked to no avail; he was aimed at the driver's side of my car and wasn't even looking at me. I could do nothing but call on Jesus, stomp the accelerator to the floor, and hope for the best. I have no doubt that angels were there to assist me.

If I had been killed, the belief that the devil has no power except what we give him would lead some Christians to conclude that I had either somehow given the devil power to do so (perhaps by not allowing the truck to go first), or that my work on earth was complete and that God must have needed me for work in heaven. Some may even say, "We can never understand the ways of God; they are past finding out."

These are just a few examples of the many fabrications of well-meaning words that actually undermine God's will and His word. I believe my narrow escape was the result of my resolve to live and move in the shelter of God's peace. Rather than rushing out the door anxiously that morning, I had waited to go out in peace, believing in God's protection.

Selwyn Hughes once wrote in his devotional Everyday with Jesus: "Is there a personal devil? Many have tried to minimize it, but the concept of a personal devil is everywhere in scripture. This is why he is called by so many appellations: liar, deceiver, murderer, accuser, tempter, prince of the power of the air, etc. He dogs the steps of the toiling saint and spreads a net for his weary feet. His business is carried on every day. He believes in you."

It is not only necessary and appropriate to have a right concept about God and His ways, but also about the devil and his. God has made a covenant with those who dare to believe. And, whether in thought or in practice, His covenant can be rendered ineffective by tradition, just as it was in Jesus' day. Furthermore, if we are not aware of the enemy's tactics, we can position ourselves to receive all that he wants for us. We live in a dangerous world that continues its spiral into chaos and lawlessness day by day. Our ignorance of the devil's tactics is largely the result of what we have heard, learned, and come to accept from what we have commonly called church.

We would like to think of church as a safe place, where a shepherd watches over us and guides us within the safe parameters of our beliefs. Unfortunately, this is a denial of what we hear, see, and experience every day. Regardless of denomination, church leaders slip into corruption, abuse and misuse of the power we give them.

A casual reading of the works of Jesus and the first-generation apostles indicates that God continued to do new things in new ways every new day. Did He stop when the Church became "organized" in the name of doing things "decently and in order" (1 Corinthians 14:40)? More importantly, does His work stop when we, in our gatherings, fall into an organized, comfortable way of doing things?

While some individuals recognize the absence of the power of God in our meetings, many do not. In fact, they want the traditions more than they want God and His power, and they easily confuse the two. Traditions don't have to be centuries or even decades old to be powerless. They must merely be important enough to us that we choose them over following the

Spirit of God. Hence, they gradually and effectively replace the fresh, living direction of His Holy Spirit.

Still, we cling to format — whether in the form of a hymn book, a homily, or a twenty-minute set of contemporary worship songs leading up to an offering. Rarely is there even a pause for the Spirit of God to speak. And if, by chance, there is a moment for the Spirit to give utterance, someone — usually the pastor — has been pre-appointed to decide whether the word is of God. Frequently, this means that if the word doesn't sound "holy," it is rejected without regard for its content.

In this 12th Anniversary edition of Cafeteria Covenant, by the refining process of the Almighty, I continue to assert that God wants to display His power in us and through us in ways we have previously only dreamed about. It is my sincere hope that each of us who have been adopted into this eternal family will realize our place in His body and allow Him to display His power through us.

For in the same way that one body has so many different parts, each with different functions; we, too—the many—are different parts that form one body in the Anointed One. Each one of us is joined with one another, and we become together what we could not be alone. Since our gifts vary depending on the grace poured out on each of us, it is important that we exercise the gifts we have been given... (Romans 12:4–8).

Looking back, I see that God's refining work has been the theme not only of this book, but of my life. Looking forward, I believe this message is more urgent now than ever. May this 12th Anniversary Edition stir you to listen for His voice, to let go of traditions that nullify His covenant, and to take your place at the table of His body — until the day we gather for the true banquet, the Marriage Supper of the Lamb.

Part One

The Journey

1

BACK AND FORTH

It had not occurred to me that a book outlining a code for modern civil behavior would have a chapter on self-esteem, much less the answer to a prayer request about writing a book. Nevertheless, citing an example of a young woman in an abusive relationship, reluctant to be assertive because she thinks it may be rude and hurtful, P.M. Forni highlights a frequently overlooked viewpoint: that if we do not consider ourselves valuable, we will have nothing to offer society in general.

"Sensitive to the feelings of others, but lacking in self-esteem," he writes, "she cannot bring herself to utter the unequivocal words to end her relationship with her self-serving and abusive boyfriend."[7]

I had been using the book to model reading to my class, while building background knowledge for a service-learning project. They were barely paying attention. My heart began to beat loudly, and with a

---

7 Ibid, p. 111

brief pause to check for God's peace, I looked up from the book and began to speak extemporaneously.

"I'm going to stop here for a minute to share a text-to-real life connection with you.[8] I want to tell you a story." They peered at me sleepily. "When I was 21, I married a man I had only known for six weeks."

I wasn't sure how this was going to end, but if I'd stayed up all night trying, I couldn't have thought of a better way to get their attention. It certainly wasn't in the lesson plan, nor was it what they expected to hear, but it certainly brought the book to life for them.

"That's dumb," one of them called out.

"What? Why?" others questioned. They were surprised by this news from their notoriously conservative teacher.

"Because," I continued, "He was the only man I'd met who showed any interest in being a father to my 3-year old daughter." They were dumbfounded.

"But the problem," I continued, "was that he was an alcoholic, and I didn't know that."

In this, a public school, I had to omit some of the details, but I proceeded to tell my students that as a young adult, I'd been rather independent and

---

8 A reading comprehension strategy in which the reader connects what she is reading to something in her own life.

assertive. I had been a single, self-supporting mother for almost three years at the very height of the women's liberation revolution before getting married.

Married life was not at all blissful, but it did cause me to cry out to God for His help. Then, we got involved in church and I learned that God hated divorce. I wanted to make sure I didn't do anything else that God hated, so I did what I could to make it work.

I did not tell my students that every time I sought counsel from the church leaders, a finger pointed back at me for not being a more "submissive" wife. I was told I was too independent and that it was making him insecure. I was reprimanded because it wasn't right to talk about him when he wasn't there to defend himself. I was advised to try to remember what our relationship was like in the beginning, which would help me to focus on the good things. What relationship? I would silently question.

I did not tell my students that because God hates divorce so much, not one counselor in fifteen years suggested that I leave my husband, although I did try it once in spite of them all. I was sent back to "try again," because it was reported that he was "truly sorry." I reasoned that if it pleased God to use me to draw this man called my husband into a deeper relationship with God, I would humbly submit.

What I did tell my students was that fifteen years later, exhausted and debilitated with pain, I decided whatever had been wrong with me for more than 24 hours could go ahead and kill me. I went to bed believing I might not wake up and all my agony would finally be over. Several hours later, I broke down and asked my irritated spouse to take me to the emergency room and he grudgingly complied. I had acute appendicitis.

"A healthy attention to our own needs" is essential to civility, Forni wrote. He follows with suggestions for establishing personal boundaries. For example, what to say to a partner who wants to smooth over an argument and just "drop it," without hearing what you really think is important. All good advice, of course, but if I had read it back in the day, I wouldn't have been able to accept any of it.

I was only interested in doing what God wanted and being acceptable among my fellow believers, regardless of how society might view it. I believed what I'd been taught, both explicitly and implicitly in church after church. As such, the most important qualification for being "accepted in the beloved," was to stay married "till-death-do-us-part."

The bottom line for me was that I would no longer be acceptable to God if I got a divorce, and even if He understood and forgave me, I would never be fit for the ministry to which He had called me. Therefore, I had to make the marriage work.

I learned to avoid confrontation whenever and however I could. No matter what other negative, abusive, or unholy things I was subjected to, I adopted the goal to show everyone what God could do with a mismatched, miserable marriage. I clung desperately to the Old Testament model of Sarah, who obeyed Abraham and called him Lord, even when he tried to dismiss her as his sister to save his own skin... twice.

Four days after my appendectomy, "Abraham" picked me up from the hospital, deposited me at home, and left... to get my pain medicine. Several hours later, he returned angry and drunk. He stomped up the stairs, yelling as he came, picked up the corner of my great-grandmother's antique bed with me lying in it, and began shaking it violently. Fearful, in a good deal of pain, and unable to run, I gave up any hope of ministry and called the police. After his arrest, when he tried to return, I gave him the choice to stop drinking or leave. He chose to depart.

I ended my truncated story that day in my classroom with a warning: "Civility begins with your personal choices. You can't just go along with things to be accepted," I continued. "You have to care enough about yourself to make the right choices."

It had been a significant teaching moment for them, but because of its timing it was even more significant for me. For about a month, I had been tending a wound inflicted by a local church leader. After hearing that I had stayed in an abusive marriage for fifteen years, she commented that the reason for this was undoubtedly my lack of self-esteem. Now, of course, Forni was saying the same thing.

On the surface of it, there was some truth to her judgment, but her remark had wounded me deeply and I was still applying Holy Ghost ointment to prevent infection. It implied that my self-sacrifice, superimposed as an essential to serving God by religious leaders twenty-five years earlier, was now a thing to be viewed with condescension. Not having self-esteem was a by-product.

A month after this incident, I was speaking to a young pastor about the call of God on his ministry, and he suggested I write a book. Since he knew nothing about me, having met me only a few minutes before, I received his suggestion as a word of spiritual encouragement.

So it was that I began to pray about how to start a book writing project, and especially where to start it. Evidently, my answer had arrived, and the book you now hold is the evidence.

2

ARTIFICIAL FLOWERS

My relationship with Jesus had sustained me through many dark years, but at the same time, my testimony had been stifled by my own questioning heart. *What could anyone possibly see in my life that would make him or her want to know God?*

Even though I realized the marriage I had been trying to preserve was no more glorifying to God than a divorce would be, I was still devastated. I sat on a park swing one cold, rainy night during my recovery, telling God that if He couldn't use me, to please just take me home. I had invested fifteen years, and it had ended in failure. My little girl was now almost eighteen, so, I reasoned, she didn't need me anymore.

Softly, tenderly, and unmistakably, the words arose from somewhere within me, "If you die, all those songs will die with you."

"Those songs…" were the precious gifts God had given me from the first day I had come to know Him. They came in words of praise, prayer, admonition and encouragement. They came with melodies and with little effort on my part except to give them voice. In fact, if I had to work at writing a song, I felt like I was cheating. I believed they were given for the edification of the body of Christ. Yet, until that time, very few people had heard any of them. It wasn't that I didn't want to share them; it's just that there was little opportunity to do so.

Now, in just ten words, God had restored me and given me a mission. I had a reason to rejoice. It was the first time I had ever *heard* His voice. Those words were sufficient to sustain me with a purpose. Since then, I had many occasions to question whether there was any purpose for the music of my soul, but each time, like a dormant seed in due season, hope would re-emerge.

I made many attempts to join with the singers and musicians of the various churches we attended over the fifteen years of our marriage. But in every case, an authority figure would discern something unsuitable in my motivation. Some would note my husband's stifling watchfulness and direct me to work on my marriage before I could "minister."

One elder told me I had spirits of pride, self-pity, and rejection from which I needed deliverance before I could be considered for *any* kind of ministry. Eager to be free of these things, I asked them to meet with me for prayer. Their response was, "We'll get back to you." After several weeks of waiting for a call, I gave up and moved on.

Over the years there were times when I told the Lord straight out, "If that's all they see in me, then I don't want to do this anymore." There seemed to be no encouragement anywhere, much less any offer of help with musical accompaniment. I didn't play any instruments. Some sweet saints would say that my voice alone was an instrument, while others suggested I learn to accompany myself (as if I had not tried).

Yet, shortly after hearing God speak to me about the songs, the provision came. A former business associate was opening a recording studio and showed an interest in using his skills on some of my music. With his accompaniments, we recorded my first album.[9]

I began to relish the freedom to do whatever I desired to do for the first time in my entire life. Among my first choices for destinations was an overflowing church I'd been curious about for several

9 *Bigger Shoes* © 1990, Dee Marvin Emeigh

months. A mere six weeks after my arrival there, the pastor asked me to join him and his wife on the platform to lead worship. It had been fifteen years since I had acknowledged Jesus as my savior and liberator. As I finally began to live in that freedom, it seemed like I was living someone else's life.

Financially, my own life was still very real to me. My employment history had consisted of intermittent stints at whatever "Abraham" would deem as "a nice little job." My devotion had been to the office of Godly wife and mother. His was to have been the breadwinner, although he was not very successful in that role. If my job required more of my time and energy than he did, the tension would increase until I had to quit.

Now needing to be self-supporting, my only prospect was a McDonald's within walking distance of the apartment where we lived, so I started there. A few months later, I was able to purchase a car for dependable transportation. Then, I boldly applied for a position that made use of my only real marketable skill.

Both in high school and again while earning my associate degree, my father had urged me to take a typing class. Despite my lack of any desire to be a secretary, which was one of only three jobs a woman could seriously consider at the time, I complied. Consequently, I was able to pass the typing test for a job to learn typesetting for a publishing company. (Thanks, Dad!) I became one of the first in the company to learn Desktop Publishing on Windows. The following year I was offered a position at another company composing layouts and typesetting their books.

In just over a year, I had progressed from making minimum wage to tripling my income and receiving benefits. Although there were still some gut-wrenching events involving my daughter, things seemed better than I could have imagined.

In the church, however, I began to notice the presence of artificial flowers. And while I didn't want to see them, think about them, or believe they were real, their twisting tendrils had already begun to wrap themselves around my ankles.

3

BUTTERFLY CHRISTIANITY

I didn't want to acknowledge the vines (or perhaps they were just microphone cords) that held me to the platform at the 600-plus member church where I had emerged. For one thing, I didn't want to be labeled a Butterfly Christian. It was said that a "Butterfly Christian," would go from one pretty bush to another, drinking in what was pleasing and then moving on to the next place. The allegory was intended to admonish believers to form lasting relationships of accountability so growth could take place.

The other, far more subtle, reason for not wanting to see it was finally being able to do what I believed I had been called to do. In fact, the first day I appeared on the platform to sing, a prophetic word from a well-respected man of God there confirmed, "This is the field I have called you to." I was where I wanted to be and where I believed God wanted me and that felt very good.

Soon, however, the pastor's wife began to suggest that I become acquainted with a man in the church. She didn't know he already had my phone number. That was because her pastor-husband had encouraged the congregation to get to know the people who sat near them in church each Sunday. I was actually quite shaken when the phone number I had obediently provided was put to use by the man who sat near me. He called to invite me to attend a Full Gospel Businessmen's Fellowship dinner. I had no interest in any kind of relationship with him or anyone else, but I didn't want to be rude. So I agreed to go, but only if I could meet him there.

Following the dinner, we met some of his friends for coffee. One of them was the president of the local FGBFI chapter. I felt relaxed enough to ask if anyone knew of a reputable repairman who could fix my clothes dryer, which had broken just that day.

"Don't you think you should go over and fix the dryer for the lady?" his friend coaxed. I had asked for help; now that it was being offered, what was I supposed to say? No, thank you. The Lord will provide!?

I prepared a meal to thank my new friend and discovered that I enjoyed his company and his respectful behavior. He was a hard-working businessman with strict Christian principles and so, feeling safe enough, I began to let down my guard.

We had begun to grow fond of doing things together when the pastor's wife discovered that my divorce from "Abraham" was not yet final. So she told me I shouldn't be seeing him. Thereafter, we would talk on the phone and meet privately. When my divorce was final, he asked me to marry him.

I could see that this met with happy endorsement from the pastor and his wife, and I thought it would put me in a more secure position in the church. I also began to receive invitations to sing at FGBFI events.

After being deprived of approval and enjoyment for so long, I assumed that it was all good and never even considered asking God about His thoughts. No one else suggested that I do so, either. Furthermore, I felt that if I did not marry this man, I would lose all I had waited so long to receive.

Forcing all my doubts to the background, I reasoned that things would be even better once we were married and free to know one another more openly and fully. A few of my family members told me they didn't think it was wise, but since they didn't know him and didn't understand my motivation, I disregarded their advice.

It did not take long for the battle of regret to rage against my self-esteem once more. If I could have faced it, I would have realized how hasty and ill-founded my decision had been. When we returned from our three-day honeymoon he announced, "Now I have to get back to the things I've been neglecting in my business." My heart felt like it would burst.

I sought the counsel of the prophet and his wife, who often taught at marriage seminars. During our conversation, the wife asked if I'd be interested in writing a couple of songs for the Easter Cantata. It eased some of the pain by renewing my focus. In a few days, I had written two songs and was working on the third, which was to be Mary's song at the tomb on Resurrection morning.

In the middle of this, I began to notice something else I tried to ignore. During worship team rehearsals, a contentious banter between the pastor and his wife often erupted into unkind remarks and tears. I attributed this to the pressure of being in a demanding ministry while trying to rear two small children. When rumors about the pastor and his secretary began to emerge, I dismissed them as gossip, believing that my job was to love them unconditionally.

Then, just before the first rehearsal for the Easter Cantata, the prophet and his wife announced they were leaving the church and moving to another city. Within weeks, the pastor stepped down from the pulpit, confessing that he had acted in a way that was unbecoming of a minister of the gospel and I later discovered that not only had he been unfaithful, but his wife had been as well.

The church elders determined it would be better for the congregation not to know what had really happened, but I argued that the truth was better than a lie. Guest speakers were summoned, and a new worship leader was selected. As the guest pastors were brought in to be voted upon, the congregation began to slip away and so did I. The happy little garden where I had come to life again was dying.

Forced out by my conviction that truth, as heart-breaking as it may be, is better than a lie that God could not honor, I began to search for another place to worship. And, while I prayed for God's guidance, I realize now that I didn't fully believe I would receive it. Only after years of humble hindsight can I see the purpose through the pain. Facing the truth was as difficult for me as it had been for the elders. If I admitted my mistake, what would be the result?

I hoped that God in His mercy would spare me from being a stained black sheep grazing on His Holy

Hill. He knew my heart was simply to be right with Him and to serve Him, and I knew He was capable of changing hearts and making even what was meant for evil into something good.[10]

---

10 Genesis 50:20

4

FLY AWAY

In the quest for a new church home, we could not ignore the little church at the bottom of the hill where we lived. The preacher was a sincere man of God, his wife a perfect hostess, and being that almost everyone was Italian, the food was always good. The music, however, did not reflect this. In fact, not long after we arrived, the pastor, who recognized me from FGBFI events, asked if I could help them transition from the traditional series of hymn-singing to a more contemporary worship style.

Thinking this was an answer from God, I embraced what I truly had no idea how to do. That was the way God always worked, wasn't it? He would choose a willing vessel and give him or her a job that could only be completed with His help.

With striking similarity to many other choices that seemed right, but in which I was only guessing at God's plan, I accepted the call. I met every obstacle with as much courage and grace as I could manage.

Starting with what they knew and what I knew, I focused on compiling songs that transitioned harmoniously from one to the next. I mixed traditional and contemporary songs that many of the people could recognize. Since the musicians all read music, I found sheet music for the songs I wanted to introduce. The congregation and the pastor seemed to respond positively, but one rather important person did not.

Each rehearsal brought more challenges and more animosity from the current worship leader, who was also the pastor's sister-in-law.

It never occurred to me that someone who had done this her own way for so long wasn't looking for a change, much less welcoming it. Although I had seen plenty of evidence to the contrary, I still believed that anything God wanted, His people would also want, and even if they didn't, they would still obey Him. Of course, I was assuming that the musical transition was what God wanted.

Called into a meeting to address the noticeable tension I had attempted to ignore, I did the only thing I knew how to do: I walked out with no explanation. The instinct to flee from trouble was well-developed, especially when I had no mandate to stay and the battle wasn't really mine. It appeared as if I had stepped into the middle of yet another domestic dispute, something for which I had more aptitude than tolerance.

Some of the Christians I knew from other places gravitated to a well-attended, non-denominational church in a nearby town and it became a safe harbor for me for a while. Home fellowship groups were a vital part of their organization and loosely modeled after the Korean experience of Reverend Cho.

I had cut my spiritual teeth in a home fellowship group many years earlier, so I was eager to participate. I was promptly directed to my home group. If I were to draw a comparison between this and my earlier experience, there would be only one thing in the common: refreshments.

Where there had been a spirit of liberty in the first group, this gathering was stifled and dispirited. The authorized topic of discussion was the pastor's morning message; the music was pre-selected by the home group leaders; the discussion was confined by their moderation. Nevertheless, if I wanted to become more involved in the larger church, this home fellowship experience was a requisite. The pastor relied on the reports he received from the fellowship leaders about the spiritual health and attitude of the sheep.

I wanted a good reputation among my fellow Christians and desired to use my gifts to contribute to the edification of the body, so I set aside my personal feelings and followed along. I even wrote a song for the church, capturing the heart of the messages at the time.

When I told the pastor about the song, he sent me to the worship director who, without hearing the song, informed me that I needed to be part of the choir before I could share any music.

At the first rehearsal, I was placed on the second row of the platform, directly behind the worship director's wife. She was easily five inches taller than I am. This, of course, made it impossible to see the director, which I ever so politely mentioned.

Even now, it is hard to believe his wife's response. "What do you need to see him for?" I was stunned, but replied without a moment's hesitation, "Because he's the director." It had no effect, so I did my best to follow along. After a few weeks of this, I tried once again to pitch the song.

Once again without even hearing the song, the director responded, "Not every song is for the congregation. Sometimes God gives you songs just for you." Stunned again, but willing to contemplate this perspective, I began to re-examine *every* song I'd ever written. I quit going to choir practice, because it was not something I really wanted to do, and if the songs really were just for me, there wasn't much point in staying. I was already weary of the trendy music and feeling a bit mistreated.

When the "Toronto Blessing" made its way through New England, I watched from the balcony. I tried to accept what was going on, even going up to the platform to test the phenomenon for myself, but I had heartfelt reservations.

The Lord spoke to me several times during the following weeks of services. Although prophetic words were fairly common events there, what I had to say did not seem to "fit" with what was occurring. All the messages He gave me were about His love. I began to wonder if I really was the one not hearing properly.

One Sunday morning one of the elders, who had become a trusted friend, met me in the parking lot before service. He warned me that the other elders had decided I would be asked to leave if I came to the platform to deliver "a word from God" again. We said goodbye in the parking lot and I departed. In the months that followed, came news of nervous breakdowns, and family as well as financial disasters within the congregation, followed by a significant decline in attendance.

5

TREASURES OF DARKNESS

A few weeks later, I received a call from another young pastor asking if I could help him by leading worship at his new church. Of course, I considered the timing to be perfect.

This pastor and his wife had servant hearts. They had completed training in a well-known Bible institute and believed it was time to step up and start a new church in the ashes of two regional church disasters.

They had recently attended a convention in another town where they had encountered a prophet whose accuracy and knowledge of scripture was so impressive they invited him to their first Sunday meeting.

He arrived with a traveling companion and sat with his eyes closed during the opening music and remarks. Then, he stood up to speak.

With compelling confidence and astounding accuracy, he called people up, speaking over them about things only they themselves knew. He shared insight and wisdom in a way I had never before witnessed. He brought gifts of books and audio teaching materials.

Every week he came, following the same pattern.

He introduced us to internationally renowned Bible teachers. I had heard some of them before, but now their teaching had new clarity. I experienced a revival in my own faith. Here at last was someone who knew the ways and the words of God, who ministered in the power of the Spirit of God, and who recognized the gifts in my life.

Inevitably, trouble erupted between the pastor's wife and the prophet, so he was asked to leave. I paid little attention to the gathering storm clouds and asked my husband if we could have the meetings in our home. He agreed, but it was short lived. He didn't like having his space invaded.

I had always wanted to have a home big enough to share with other Christians in fellowship. Now that I had one, but could not share it, I was despondent. What was left of this, my second marriage, began to deteriorate dramatically. The meetings were held in someone else's home, and I began staying there for hours on end, studying, reading, and growing in my faith, going home only to sleep.

The prophet continued to come, guiding us in developing a mission: We would purchase Bibles, books, and teaching materials from the ministries we supported and give them away to individuals we met. By distributing these materials, we would spread the life-changing message we were receiving without any cost to the recipients.

As noble as the mission was, the more I became acquainted with the prophet, the more I was obliged to overlook. He had some very disturbing personal habits and could be quite critical and cruel. He often berated my vocal ability and criticized my motivation whenever I tried to sing.

One day, as I stood up to share a new song God had put in my heart, he came face-to-face with me, screaming that I was not a "real" servant of God. Already withering, what remained of my confidence, motivation to sing, and the wellspring of my songwriting, dried up.

Others had joined the group because of my influence, and I reasoned that as long as they were being brought to the knowledge of liberating truth, it did not matter that I was sacrificed in the process. At least I knew how to survive it. My heart's desire was to see the work become all it could and should have been, and to have others learn what I was learning about faith in the Word of God. Yet, little by little, because of the prophet's increasing authoritarian manner, the others began to break away. There was so much wrong, but I wanted to make it right. Soon only four of us remained and, although no one else knew it, I was being subjected to more physical abuse.

When my daughter, now living in another state, went into premature labor with her third child, I went to help her. Although the baby did not survive, I believed I was supposed to stay with her, and she and her husband graciously took me in.

Hoping to break away from the mission and start fresh, I asked for some of the books and teaching materials I had helped to purchase, but my request was denied. The prophet had become more manipulative, overbearing, and relentless over time, now even sowing discord between my daughter and me. Finally, my son-in-law asked me to leave their home, so I began to look for a place to go immediately.

My marriage was irreconcilable, and I let my husband have the condo. I had waited, wept, watched, and prayed. My credit card debt for the mission was over $20,000. I was in a new state, with a new job, but I knew no one. I could not look back or down, to the left or right. I could only put one foot in front of the other, my hand in the hand of Almighty God and believe, like never before, that I could really hear Him clearly, as He had promised in His word, "My sheep hear my voice and the voice of another they will not follow" (John 10:27).

After one final, grueling trip through sleet, freezing rain, and snow back to the mission community to complete some unfinished business, I left quietly without saying goodbye to anyone. The next day at work the phone rang. I caught my breath when I heard his voice.

"Are you coming back?"

I held my breath and managed to utter a firm, "No." Then I hung up the phone. As I did, the words rose up from deep within, "Out on dry ground." I had crossed through a virtual Red Sea, leaving everything behind. I was free again.

6

CORNELIUS[11]

Painfully aware of the damage that had been done to other people's lives and, more importantly, to their faith, I resolved to make it my ambition to lead a quiet, solitary life. I could not bear to hurt anyone else or be hurt myself. I knew God was with me and that He would provide.

A new level of liberty had arrived, to follow Him as I believed He was leading. Every day on my way to work, I passed a handyman special on a piece of country property where the nearest neighbors were Amish. As a first-time home buyer, I learned I could qualify for a special $1000-down mortgage. But, I would have to believe God to provide handymen, because what the house needed was far beyond my own ability to fix.

About that time, my supervisor sent me across town to ask a local newspaper photographer if he

---

11   Acts 10

could take some photos for our publication. We met a few times to discuss the project. "Where do you go to church?" he asked me one day. He said he was asking because he could see that I really believed what I said.

I didn't want to lead him or anyone else in any direction but to the throne of God's great grace. It had been ten years since anyone had asked where I went to church. Oddly enough, it was during another time when I had no place to call "my church," that a visually impaired boy had wanted to know.

"The church without walls," I had told him.

"Where's that?" the young man asked.

"It's right here, right now as you and I are talking, because Jesus said, 'wherever two or more of you gather together, I am there with you.'"

This time, however, I knew the question required a more substantive answer.

"Why do you ask?" I replied.

"Just curious. I thought I would go with you sometime."

"I really don't have a church to go to, but I believe that Jesus lives in me, and I try to take direction from Him in all I do."

Gary's questions were courteous and genuine. Because of my convictions, he had ruled out any possibility of being anything more than a friend, but it was quite evident that I needed a friend.

The little house needed extensive work before it would be comfortably livable. The realtor had promised to do the repairs or find someone to do them, but his stalling tactics included persistent invitations to dinner and contrived reasons to stop by his lovely home to retrieve papers or to show me what he had done there, all the while producing none of the promised work.

Now under contract as a lease with option to buy, I asked Gary if he could take a look at the house. He confided in me later that he had said to himself, 'This is nothing I want to get involved in.' But, what he actually said to me was, "You can call that realtor and tell him you don't need his help. I have a lot of friends, and I think we can get this done. Until then, I have a spare room at my house that can be your sanctuary if you want it. No strings."

Tears welled up in my eyes as he told me about his network of friends that would drop everything to help one another. They came from all walks and professions: lawyers, teachers, police officers, journalists, carpenters, and electricians. It sounded as if they were to each other what the Church should be, and Gary sounded like what every Christian should be.

"Do you believe in God?" I asked him.

He answered by telling me of his early experience with religion, which ended in despicable abuse of power by nuns at a Catholic school. His mother had removed her children and never sent them back to the school or to the church. He could not understand how they could represent God and be so mean. I couldn't either.

He had already told me stories of his amazing close encounters with death: surviving a mid-air collision in a small plane and a brain tumor that threatened to take his eyesight, if not kill him. Tales of his younger days compared to the person he was now made it obvious that decisions and adjustments he made along the way had changed him. And while he never completely answered my question, he did acknowledge he believed there was some superior being. Then he asked me, "Would it make a difference whether I believe the same way you do or not?"

God, what kind of a question is this? What kind of an answer do I give someone who acts more like a Christian than anyone I've met in my 25 years of being in churches?

I knew God's love did not depend on whether we love Him or not. We love Him because He first loved us. It is His goodness that leads others to Him in repentance. And so, in yet another step across yet another boundary of conviction, I answered, "No."

In the weeks that followed, Gary made it his mission not only to enlist the aid of all of his friends –

"Hey Mike, it's been a long time. How are you doing? Yeah, we need to get together. What are you doing this Saturday? Great! Bring a hammer!"

– but also to bring my family back together.

"Why don't you ask your family to come over for some hamburgers Sunday?"

It was a long and painful process. I loved my family with my life, but I had lost them in my pursuit of what I thought was pleasing to God. I was more certain than ever of God's voice, His guidance, and of my own unworthiness. And, while I wanted Gary to know God through the narrow door, it appeared as if God already knew him. "I can work with him," the Lord said to me. There was no doubt about that.

My stepmother, who visited with my dad just after the house was completed, said it best, "If you hadn't met Gary, you would have been a hermit."

When my dad passed away a year later, it was Gary who put me on the plane and met me with open arms on my return. When a new supervisor restructured my job and insisted that anything less than unquestioned obedience was insubordination, it was Gary who encouraged me to pursue freelance photojournalism, and then taught me everything I needed to know.

When my mother and stepfather were unable to take care of themselves the following year, it was Gary who helped me move them from New York to Delaware.

When my mom lashed out at me in her dementia, it was Gary who calmed her down.

When I wasn't on my own photo assignments, I was with Gary on his.

It was on one of these assignments that I discovered a Christian theater group and soon became involved. I was looking forward to my mom and stepfather being in the audience for my leading role in the Christmas show, but just after rehearsals began, my mother had a massive stroke and died.

Two weeks later, it was my stepfather who departed this life. And again, it was Gary who was there to hold me together.

On opening night in the dressing room, the young woman who was cast in the role of my daughter in the show, Four Tickets to Christmas, asked if my family was going to be there. "My mom and stepfather were supposed to be here," I said, "But they both passed away during rehearsals."

She looked into my eyes and reached for my hands. "They'll be here," she said resolutely. "They have front row seats!" She hugged me as the tears flowed between us. I had so wanted them to see that my life had finally turned around. They had all watched me go through one horrid experience after another, but they had not lived to see the positive outcome.

Her words so inspired me that when the show was over, I sat down the next night and wrote the script for an autobiographical musical framed in the Resurrection story. Using songs I'd already written as well as other readily available music, the theater company scheduled it as the Easter show. I directed and performed in the musical, and the unfinished song from the unfinished cantata of a decade earlier, "Mary's Song," came to life at last, becoming the title song of the show, Wings! It seemed that my life was starting to make some sense.

7

WINGS!

Wings! was in final rehearsals, and Gary and I were quietly planning a life together, when he flew a plane to Virginia with a reporter to cover a college basketball game. He called to let me know they would be staying another night. A few hours later, I was awakened from a sound sleep by another call. I did not recognize the voice.

"Something terrible has happened."

"Who is this?"

"It's Gary. Something terrible has happened." The voice was hoarse and shaking.

The reporter had changed his mind, wanting to come back to Delaware and return to the tournament the next day. They had gone to the airport where, in a series of events that only made sense after the FAA investigation, he had walked into the propeller of the Cessna 172 and was instantly killed. Gary was traumatized.

Six weeks later, Gary's father passed away. We had been planning a wedding trip to visit him in New Newfoundland. Although Gary said I was there for him, I felt inadequate to console him. He immersed himself in his work, refusing to talk to anyone about it. We postponed our wedding until the fall.

As the months passed, it became apparent that while I desired to do for him all he had done for me, I was helpless to accomplish it. My earnest prayer became his restoration. In part, this was born of selfish desire; I wanted our life to go on as it had been before. Now, so much of him was wounded; he had lost so much, and I wanted him to know God's goodness, His comfort, and His peace.

"Lord, please don't let this stop him from flying. Don't allow this to be taken away from him too," I prayed. A few days later, Gary met an old acquaintance who asked if he was still flying.

"Not much," he replied sadly. The man invited him to become a pilot for the Civil Air Patrol (United States Air Force Auxiliary). My unselfish prayer was answered; my selfish one was not.

Gary would continue to bear in his soul the scars of that spring. Furthermore, almost a year later, a member of the reporter's family filed a lawsuit against him that lasted for several years, adding more sorrow and grief to his already wounded heart.

There seemed to be nothing I could do to relieve him of his despair, even for a few hours. All I knew to do was draw nearer to God myself and continue to pray for God's goodness to be manifest to him. I prayed and confessed the promises of God's Word over him while seeking guidance and believing that I received it for myself. I had to learn how to love this new version of Gary as much as I had loved the old one, giving him space and time to heal, and accepting a new, unwanted plan for life.

When the stock market fraud of the early twenty-first century resulted in the loss of all the investments I had planned to use for retirement, the need for another new plan became more evident. Contributing to that was a 90% decline in my freelance photography work due to management changes at the newspaper that provided the bulk of my work.

These things were foremost in my prayers and thoughts, but I could not see any logical next step. At about that time. Gary's youngest daughter was graduating from college, engaged to be married, and looking forward to beginning her first job as a teacher. Over a celebratory dinner, her dad and fiancé were teasing that her motivation for being a teacher was so that she could have summers off. In an effort to build rapport with her, I leaned across the restaurant booth and reassured her, "I wanted to be a teacher once."

I was surprised that Gary had even heard me. "What would it take for you to do that?" he asked.

"I'd have to go back to school."

"Well, why don't you look into that?"

Simple. At least, it sounded simple. As I had prayed, the thought of teaching had surfaced more times than I was willing to admit, but I didn't consider it possible. When I was younger, I didn't think I was smart enough. I had struggled in every subject but English and art, so I had taken courses that would guarantee my success.

After high school and completion of my associate degree, I had jumped into the workforce to support a one-year old baby. There was little time to pursue anything else.

When she was a preschooler and I was a stay-at-home mom, I had investigated the opportunity again, because at that time, certification to teach in primary grades could be obtained by adding a few additional courses to the associate degree. But loans were not available to me.

Returning to the workforce fifteen years later, I had recognized the need to continue my education, so I enrolled in occasional classes as needed. One of my many occupations as I climbed my way up from minimum wage, was teaching software applications. There, I rediscovered the passion for teaching, but not the confidence to take on the "real degree," as I called it. As I could see it now, my greatest need was faith.

Over the next few days, Gary suggested I liquidate my shrinking assets and use the finances to go back to college. I issued the order to sell immediately. A week later and there would have been nothing left.

Then came the search for a school. At one local university, the admission counselor told me I was too old to become a teacher because the school districts preferred younger, more moldable candidates. She suggested I become a respiratory therapist instead.

"But I don't want to be a respiratory therapist," I replied. So, she tried another tactic to discourage me: They would only accept a possible 18 of the 93 college credits I had earned.

She succeeded only in discouraging me from applying to her university. I believed God was directing me, so I focused my search on colleges that would accept my credits. In the process, I discovered that our state offered an alternate route to secondary teaching credentials for those who had bachelor degrees in areas of critical needs; English was one of them. Naturally, it made sense to focus on that. With each step I took, the path became more clear. Still, none of the local colleges offered the degree or the credit transfer I needed.

My only option was to investigate distance learning. On the very first phone call to inquire about a distance degree, the counselor told me he thought his organization would accept most of my credits. When he explained that my degree would be matriculated by Charter Oak State College in Connecticut, it was hard to contain my joy.

At least a decade earlier, I had seen a brochure for Charter Oak at the community college where I'd been taking coursework in technical communications. I remembered thinking it was a dream I didn't dare to dream.

Now, at age 54, when it would have seemed even more impossible to most people I knew, I began the first of eleven upper-level courses from six different colleges, local and at a distance. Each class refined my vision. I enjoyed taking the distance classes so much that I made teaching them part of my five-year plan.

Never before had I been able to plan something and actually accomplish it. Never before had I thought I was smart enough to return to college. Never before had I been able to focus beyond every distraction that would prevent me from reaching the finish line. I knew God had not just given me the vision, He was in me, empowering, guiding, and providing.

Nine months later, Gary and I drove to Connecticut so I could graduate with my bachelor's degree in literature, and just one year from the time I began my first upper-level course, the doors opened for me to teach English at a Christian high school.

The joy of my accomplishment, however, was quickly overshadowed by the realization that some of my students were struggling to read the class literature, and I didn't know how to help them. I had just completed an undergraduate research project that reported our nation's illiteracy rate was an alarming 33 percent and that literacy, crime, and poverty rates were inextricably bound together. I myself had been in remedial reading classes in fifth grade, and thereafter a struggling reader, forced to find my own way to learn. In addition, I had spent fifteen years married to someone whose lack of education and literacy skills fostered misunderstanding and hindered every learning and earning opportunity.

I was keenly motivated, but still profoundly unable to help my students. Each of these motivations, magnified by my sense of helplessness, propelled me further.

Stepping out once more on nothing but faith, I began graduate studies in reading education and second language literacy the following fall. The principal of the Christian school responded favorably to my suggestions and innovations, allowing me to set up screenings and interventions, as well as a new student choice-centered summer reading project. After completing both graduate degrees in the fall of 2009, I was offered a position as a reading intervention teacher in a public high school: yet another place I never dreamed I would be.

8

GO ON

Ironically, it was my mother's death that brought the song in my heart back to life. Unable to cope with the end of what had been a long and difficult relationship with her, my heart found expression in writing a song in her honor. It had been several years since

Still, I could not find any local help with musical accompaniment. I searched the internet for a Christian arranger and producer.

Eric Copeland had just begun a ministry to Christian singer-songwriters like me who needed to take their music to the next level. I sent him a voice recording of Window Boxes, and he went to work.

When the minister who married Gary and me heard it, he invited me to sing the song for Mother's Day. Then, the pastor at my daughter's church asked me to come. Soon, I was attending a small church that was comprised of "cell" groups and the pastor was relieved that someone had come who could lead the song service, but there were no musicians. For more than a year, I planned worship music with CD tracks and prayed for musicians to come. None did. When my family started to leave for other places, I asked to be relieved of the commitment.

My oldest granddaughter would soon be leaving for college, and I wanted to go to church where she was singing to enjoy what she was doing while I could. When she did leave, I did not feel led to stay. If one person had made an attempt to speak with me, I might have, that was not the case. I did not feel led to return to my previous post either.

"Lord, where do you want me to go?" I inquired. The answer surprised me, but I was obedient and found myself in a very large congregation, the same one Gary's first wife had been attending for many years. I reasoned that I could remain anonymous in a large congregation. No one informed God of this plan. On my very first Sunday there, my heart leaped to see an announcement for their Christmas musical auditions.

I signed away my anonymity at the audition and was given a lead role in the production. The cast members and ministry made me feel very much at home. Because I was also finishing my graduate degrees at the time, I was not in their Easter show, but I joined them again in a supporting role for the Christmas presentation the following fall.

When an opening was announced on the worship team, I enthusiastically auditioned. It took a few months to receive the results, but I was informed that another selection had been made because my voice didn't blend with the group. It stunned me. All through my school years I had sung with choirs and choruses; I had been on two or three contemporary worship teams since then, and no one had ever said this before.

As I prayed I began to see that the truth of this was more spiritual than musical. A few weeks later, I joined a secular choral group and God confirmed His Word to me through what I would have considered a very unlikely source. Without knowing what had been said to me before, the director welcomed me by saying, "Your voice would blend with anyone's."

I gave prayerful consideration to all these events: the doors closing on my involvement in any one church, the impending celebration of my 60th birthday, and still no one with whom I could really work on music.

Believing every step of the way that God was telling me to "go on," I sat down and wrote the song by that name. Eric was pleasantly surprised to hear from me again after five years, and he really liked the song. Gary and I went to Nashville that summer to record the vocal and music video.

It was encouraging to have professional musicians and friends respond favorably to a song. So much so, that I began thinking and praying about developing more of the music and recording a new album. Once I made this decision, the songs began to flow from my heart again with a confidence that couldn't be shaken. As I completed each song, I sent it to Eric. I also sent a few older songs that had never been arranged.

For so many years I had waited to be raised up in and by a local church, but that was not God's plan. I still hear it said that if someone is called to a ministry, he or she should be willing to work his or her way up to it, serving in a local church, by "cleaning the toilets." Although I had been willing to do this, the argument has no specific scriptural support. Worse yet, it forces the one with the servant heart to seek the approval of man. In my case, it never came. What did come, however, was the confidence at last that I was hearing Him say, "Go on," even if I was the only one who could hear Him.

Part Two

A New Covenant

9

EMERGING

An interesting mix of people gathered under the roof of a church in Dover, Delaware to celebrate the life of a journalist colleague. Familiar hymns and predicted responses, snippets of appropriate scripture, bagpipes, and pipe organs enveloped and sealed the sorrow of family and friends.

Later, a "newsman's lunch" at a gun club gave everyone the opportunity to remember good times. I invited the minister to sit with us. He was well-prepared to explain when I inquired about his church's branch on the denominational tree. Then he made a reciprocal inquiry about my own spiritual background.

"Sounds like you've been on quite a journey," he observed quietly.

"Indeed," I responded. "In fact, I'm not sure I fit in anywhere anymore. I just can't conform any longer to things I don't believe are right."

He asked me to explain what I believe. So, I did: I believe that we must have a personal relationship with Jesus Christ to experience the blessing of covenant with God, that the New Covenant is exactly that, a NEW covenant. The promises of the covenants of God are available on the basis of one thing: faith. It is by faith so that it can be by grace (not by our works). I further stated that evangelicals have sequestered themselves to the point of uselessness, that many are self-righteous, and that the power of God has gone missing from the church.

He was insightful. When I spoke about spending fifteen years in an abusive marriage because I wanted to please God, only to hear it said in those same evangelical circles that I stayed in the marriage because of poor self-esteem, he interjected, "As if it were your fault that you were abused." I nodded.

The conversation with the minister lasted only a few minutes, but in my soul it continued for hours and I felt compelled to write it down.

In my truly born-again heart, I am an evangelical, yet I feel quite like a rag doll spilling over the sides of the box she once was so carefully folded into. Furthermore, I've seen many new churches break away from denominations with idealistic enthusiasm, reach a certain level of "growth," and then gradually adopt the form of godliness they decried in the denominations they left.

It was not surprising to discover that this minister represented one of the more liberal denominations of protestantism. In his words, it was like "a glass of water without the glass." I speculate, but can't prove, that the liberal denominations have become such in the pursuit of being "all things to all people."[12] He wondered if I'd heard of the emergent or emerging church, so I began to research it. What emerged for me was more clarity.

Dissatisfied with what the organized church has become, the emerging or emergent church apparently takes many forms. Although it is inviting because it accepts so many expressions of worship, many of these expressions are not built on the foundation Jesus Christ set forth. This foundation is the subject of Jesus' famous statement to (Simon) Peter.

When Jesus addressed Peter saying, "You are Peter, and upon this rock I will build my Church," Jesus was laying a new foundation. However, it was not, as many believe, that Peter himself was to be the cornerstone of the Church. In the context, Jesus had been inquiring what others were saying about Him. He wanted His disciples to confirm that many were

---

12   1 Corinthians 9:22

calling Him a prophet (a returning Elijah or Jeremiah) and he wanted them to express what they believed to be true (much as the minister had done with me).

Accordingly, Jesus asked his disciples, "And you, what do you think?" Simon was the first to speak: "You are the Anointed One. You are the Son of the Living God." Jesus responded, "Simon, son of Jonah, your knowledge is a mark of blessing, for you didn't learn this truth from your friends or from teachers or from sages you've met on the way. You learned it from My Father in heaven... This is why I have called you Peter (rock): for on this rock I will build My Church" (Matthew 16).

Jesus gave Simon a new name, Peter (Rock). It was like saying, "Now, you understand and it's going to change you into a new man!" He let Peter know that this revelation or "blessing," not from friends, teachers, or sages along the way, but directly from God the Father, was the foundation on which His eternal Church would be built. Jesus told Peter the gates of hell would not prevail against His Church — the one built on the revelation of who He is.

If we are honest about the condition of the church in our day, we must admit the gates (or powers) of hell have prevailed. Could it be that Jesus' words didn't have a lasting impact, or were other things built upon the foundation He laid?

If the foundation was the revelation, by the Spirit of God, of who Jesus was and what He came to do, then even the most academic arguments of those who align with the earliest form of organized church have missed the point. For even these most noble orders are filled with every device necessary to disarm and "tame" the church into a toothless lion content to lap milk, because it does not grow to maturity and lacks the strength to chew meat. Instead, the church lives out its days within the confines of its own walls. Leaders must be able to feed the lion and help keep it alive: sing to it, stroke it, and simultaneously bring it new members that will do the same.

When I was a mere babe in Christ, I received a prophetic song that I sang only to a few people. It seemed very harsh, and I lacked the confidence to say, "Thus says the Lord," because I wanted to be sure it was not just my flesh reacting to the injustices I had experienced. More than fifty years later, it no longer seems harsh, for I have seen these things in every place where the Lord has taken me as a participating visitor. In fact, I am certain that the time has come to share it.

I see a building, a building of man,
Built on the foundation that I began.
Corrupt and decayed, though it seems so grand.
The bricks are impure with the precepts of man.

So much has been added but not by My hand.
So I will destroy it. Not one thing will stand,
Except the foundation which I will preserve.
And build it myself as I said in My word.

When I come with fire all the trash will be burned:
Wood, hay, and stubble as I have discerned.
Look out now and run from the city, My own.
Come out and be saved,
Even though you're alone.

For one day I'll gather the living stones
And fit them together as sinews and bones.
My bride, My temple, My body, My own,
Will rise up together and I'll take her home.

Another reason I did not share this song was my misguided belief that God would make even my enemies to be at peace with me as long as He was pleased with me (Proverbs 16:7). So, I also needed to be sure that the reactions, responses and treatment I received were not part of God's purposes for me. I kept seeing my enemies multiply wherever I turned, and they weren't very peaceful. Hence, I concluded that God was not pleased with me. I tried everything I could to bring peace, but it seemed they were for war. I even tried to please them, thinking that this was laying down my life for them. They used my back to walk on.

It took many years to see and believe that I simply needed to focus on pleasing God. Clearly, trying to please the enemy in an effort to be pleasing to God is a masterful deception. But now, emerging from every dark and painful experience of my life was a shimmering fiber of this truth, woven by the hand of God into a strong and beautiful tapestry: the only thing we can ever do to please God is believe, to take the seed of faith in His Word, plant it in a receptive heart, and let it grow. "Without faith no one can please God because the one coming to God must believe He exists, and He rewards those who come seeking" (Hebrews 11:6). The peace that we are promised, even with our enemies, is a peace that God establishes in us because of our relationship of faith in Him.

This peace operates as the deciding vote in our choices, and His Word, living and active within us, operates as a sharp surgical instrument to divide the soul and its thoughts and intents with those of the individual's spirit. If my motive was tainted with the response of my soul to the treatment I had received, it would not have been a pure Word from God.

In this day and time, we are hyper-vigilant to political correctness as a way to live peacefully with others, but we have grown grossly insensitive to true righteousness, even calling what is evil good and what is good evil.[13] As a society, we have interpreted peace to be complacency, sacrificing the courage to stand up for what is right in order to protect someone's feelings, and ourselves from retribution. It's as if we are saying, it's not worth the trouble to stand up for what is right; so we acquiesce when we should stand firm.

In the church we focus on minutia (gnats), while absorbing disproportionate amounts of doctrinal error (camels).[14] By our own human effort, we cannot meet the requirement of being everything to everyone. To keep us preoccupied with our

---

13 Isaiah 5:20
14 Matthew 23:24

attempt to do so, the enemy will send an endless army of those who will war against us, leading us further away from the Truth with each subsequent skirmish.

Accepting the precepts of man as doctrine is a token substitute for true relationship with God. It reduces righteousness to rules of conduct. There is only one thing that makes us right with God and capable of doing (His) good works. That is accepting, as our own, the offering Jesus has made for us, in full awareness of our own inability, no matter how hard we try or how well we perform. Living in the New Covenant requires a day-by-day acceptance of our continual need for His intervention. We can only be righteous because of His righteousness living inside of us. We need to depend on God within us every day and in every way.

10

POWER TO MATURE

We are destined to mature into the fullness of the anointing of the Anointed One (Christ) by learning to trust in His promises and responding to the leading of His voice, not by following rules, rote, and rituals. It is not a single occurrence, but a series of faithful, obedient steps in a process of growth. As such, we are not meant to merely reflect His glory as His *representa-tives*; we are meant to radiate His glory as His *representa-tions*.

The expectation that new converts or those who have not yet truly embraced the covenant Jesus initiated by faith should exhibit mature Christian behavior is ludicrous. It is like expecting a newborn to eat a five-course dinner. It can't be done. It is easier to teach them to follow rules. But rules (laws) were to be used for training purposes until the time of maturity.[15]

The ever-daily walk, and work of faith in His power alone is anything but a careless ramble of relinquished responsibility because of a belief that God is "in control." Living in Him is not an

---

15 Galatians 3:24

effortless, downstream flow of thinking that whatever comes is coming from Him. This is an abdication of our responsibility. It is not taking the "good with the bad" from God, for God is not bad.

In spite of the words of many of His followers, even those presented in the Old Testament and its covenants (who had a limited understanding because they did not have the very Spirit of God to live in them and guide them to Truth), God is not the taker of life. God is the giver and receiver of life.

It is, rather, our mortal enemy, the same who tempted and succeeded in turning Eve and Adam from the garden of God, who takes life: stealing, killing, and destroying whatever we allow. It may be through our lack of knowledge, but it is still what we allow.[16] This same mortal enemy tempted Jesus. And while Jesus defeated him and gave his followers power to overcome him, Satan is still the ruler of this world.[17]

Hence, we aren't giving the devil power. He already has it. It is important to make up our minds about God if we are ever going to receive anything from Him.

To say of someone who meets an untimely death, as I may have done that long ago day in my

16 Hosea 4:6
17 2 Corinthians 4:4

Civic, "God took her," is to say that God is not good. Deuteronomy 28 begins with the following words, spoken by Moses:

> *If you listen closely to the voice of the Eternal your God and carefully obey all the commands I'm giving you today, He'll lift you up high above every other nation on earth. All of the following blessings will be yours—in fact, they'll chase after you—if you'll listen to what He tells you (1-2).*

The blessings are clearly outlined. They don't include untimely death. That, as with many other unfortunate circumstances, falls under the category of the curse. God certainly receives those that are His because of their identity with Jesus Christ in the covenant of faith. He will also punish the wicked on the day that is established for His judgment, as He does even now by allowing them to partake of the fruit they themselves have sown. But His desire is that we be satisfied with a long life.[18]

It is God's plan and desire that we grow up in Christ – the anointing of the Anointed One. This was His purpose in establishing apostles, prophets, pastors, teachers, and evangelists. It was not simply

---

18 Psalm 91

to make us feel good temporarily or to be encouraged or revived every once in a while, nor was it an attempt to control our lives.

Each of us is destined to grow into the fullness of God's power in the anointing of His Son. The lack of power and the substitution of planned performances and programs in the modern church are largely the result of the lack of this maturity. This was observed many times on my journey as participating visitor, and the world has seen it for a very long time. As a result, many turn to other "gods" for power.

While the church desperately needs true fathers and mothers of the faith, they are rare. In fact, they are rarely found within the framework of what the church has become. They are often found outside the walls and boundaries of the church because they no longer fit its confines. The same walls and boundaries that were meant to strengthen the church have weakened and hindered it from growing and developing. Therefore, real growth into maturity is hindered.

God is more about developing us into intelligent, yielded, in-tune, mature, imaginative, free agents with whom He cooperates and communes and through whom He reconciles all things, than He is about keeping us in rule-ridden boxes that prevent our growth. He wants His bride to be as powerful and wise as her bridegroom.

So then, what is hindering the growth process?

When I was a young child, my folks took me to see a movie called The Inn of the Sixth Happiness. It was not by any means a children's movie, and I saw what I could never un-see. I have one vivid memory. I can think of no other reason why I saw and remember the following scene, except to illustrate this truth. A missionary was unwrapping the feet of the women and girls and everyone seemed very apprehensive. It was as if they were breaking some kind of a law.

I later learned that in pre-twentieth century China, women with bound feet were admired for being submissive and helpless. Often, the bones in the feet were deliberately broken to keep the feet from growing. It was a status symbol, because these women then needed servants to do everything for them. This painful process forced upon them as young girls literally crippled them to make them socially acceptable.

In reality, their feet became irreversibly deformed, frequently decayed, and occasionally gangrened and deadly. So, they were always kept perfumed and hidden, even from their high-class husbands who prized these women as faithful and sensual sexual partners because of their "lotus feet," as they were called. When medical missionaries began to work in China, the custom became known to the rest of the world, and the practice of binding feet fell into the disfavor it so rightfully deserved.

What kept this tradition alive for so long? The women were crippled in order to provide their husbands with peace of mind that they were chaste and unable to compete with them as providers. Another word for this is helpless. It was intuitively known that the feet were no longer beautiful, as they had been in their natural form, but the position of subjection necessitated by their disability was more highly prized than their health or natural beauty.

This is analogous to Satan's intentions for the Church through the use of enslaving customs and traditions. He desires to keep her powerless to serve, shamefully hiding her deformity behind a façade of wonderful performance with no soul, and unable to deliver the power she was meant to wield. He knows that the true children of God are the ones who are led by God's Holy Spirit,[19] even if they themselves do not realize it. And he will battle tirelessly to keep them from learning that truth.

Consider the imagery in the following passage from Isaiah, 52:7: "How beautiful on the mountains are the feet of the messenger who brings good news,

---

19 Romans 8:14

the good news of peace and salvation, the news that the God of Israel reigns" (New Living Translation). The good news of God's reign is carried on strong, agile feet that can walk across the mountains and out into the marketplace! Those beautiful feet are not crippled and deformed. They are unbound. They are free to go wherever they desire, and they desire to go God's way. The good news brings with it the fresh mountain air, not the stench of decay!

God designed us so He could live within us, to continue the works He began to display through His son in new, creative ways. He desires to display His goodness out in the open to all, not in dead customs that emulate holiness, or behind walls that keep His power constrained and His glory hidden!

I have frequently heard it said that God does what He wants to do on the earth and that He's in control of everything. This is why so many blame Him when things go wrong. Of course, ultimately, times and seasons are in His Hands. In the end, we will see this. Meanwhile, we have far more to do with what God does on the earth than most people, including many Christians, want to believe.

It was not easy for me to see that I could control the working of God in my life. My misconception of His will effectively blinded me. as

It is indeed quite possible to constrain God's power. Jesus' teachings tell us much about this.

Even in the one prayer all Christians know and can recite, we find Jesus saying, "Thy kingdom come, Thy will be done on earth as it is in heaven." Is it possible that even Jesus, the exact manifestation of the Father, needed to pray for the will of God and His kingdom to be revealed on the earth? If we believe that the Bible is true, we must consider this a fact. Jesus spent time praying for the will of God and His kingdom to come and He taught His disciples to do the same.

Jesus also taught about the cares and riches and worries of this life choking the Word that was sown, so that it could not bring forth mature fruit. The cares of this life, the riches, and the distractions are inevitable. How we handle them takes a commitment to leave our way behind and allow Him to work His way in us and through us. This is a matter of learning to trust Him.

Jesus referred to the Parable of the Sower, as the key to all the other parables. In fact, He told His disciples if they didn't understand this particular parable, it was unlikely they would understand any of the others.[20] Perhaps it was because they needed to embrace the truth of it, the responsibility for

20 Mark 4:3-13

maturing in faith, in order to reach a true understanding of all the other parables.

Furthermore, although Jesus healed everyone who came to Him everywhere else, He was unable to do mighty works in His own town, Nazareth. The people there did not recognize Him as anything more than the carpenter's son. He was powerless to bring them the kingdom of God because of their unbelief.[21] Before we begin to imagine that we wouldn't treat Him that way, let us consider that what we do to the least of His brothers, we do to Him.

Conversely, I have known some precious Christians in our twenty-first century American society who have attempted to take the Word of God literally and accomplish it in their own power. This can also hinder growth. In today's world, it would be unwise to advocate bringing strangers into your home; some having done so have not entertained angels but demons.[22] One group I know of took turns giving refuge to a homeless woman, and many of them are now without homes because she set fire to them. Another woman I know spent the better part of a decade berating her friends' un-Christian behavior because they did not take her in with her children. Unable to hold down a job, she regularly

21 Mark 6:6
22 Hebrews 13:2

called those who had tender hearts and extra rooms to ask for just a night on their sofas. When they agreed, she would stay until she was asked to leave.

These examples illustrate the importance of being able to hear God's voice clearly, each for ourselves, rather than to rely on our own understanding of the Word of God. God can and will speak clearly to reveal His will when we want to accomplish it. It is not just knowing the words in the Bible that is essential to our life, health and growth; it is knowing how to interpret the words by the revelation of the Holy Spirit of God. This is the same revelation (rock) to which Jesus referred. It is what makes water turn solid under our feet as we step out in faith.

As Paul admonished Timothy to do, you and I must be diligent to present ourselves approved to God as workmen who do not need to be ashamed, accurately handling the word of Truth (II Timothy 2:15, New American Standard Version). What God says may surprise us, and we must be sure we have practiced listening to Him, but He desires all His sheep to know His voice.

There is no shortcut on this journey. Maturity takes time, practice, and patience. He will begin with little things and progress to greater ones. Through the practice of listening to Him and stepping out to do the little things He shows us, we begin to gain confidence.

Time and again in my life, the voices of others drowned out the voice of God, until I determined that nothing was more important to me than the assurance of hearing Him. It meant shutting out all the distracting voices of the world as well as well-intended Christians around me. But I know that it is only as we each hear His voice and obey Him that we will begin to grow into our destiny as individuals, and corporately, as the body of believers in the world.

11

FINDING THE VOICE

Our ministry (or mission) is not about success in terms of popularity; it is about success in terms of completing what God has called us to do. If we aren't doing that, it really doesn't matter if the whole world thinks we're great. In fact, it is quite probable that the whole world won't think we're great.

Without the inner strength and conviction from God by His Holy Spirit, that what we are saying or doing is what we have heard Him say to us directly, we will have no assurance and therefore, no Divine power. This was true of the prophets and apostles, and it is true of us. How else could Paul and Silas, bound by chains in the depths of a Roman prison, sing God's praise? They didn't just think they were hearing and doing what God had directed them to do. If that were the case, they would have been weeping and wondering if they'd missed God. Rather, they knew they had heard from God and this knowledge and assurance comforted and empowered them.

In the first few months of my walk with God, I heard His voice, but I didn't have confidence in it. A large portion of the reason for this was the response I received from trusted members of the church. Sixty years later, I can clearly see that their hearts were filled with jealousy that I, a new believer, could be hearing from God when they evidently were not. While I was repelled and hurt by their responses, I had no strength or knowledge to argue my case. Instead, the Holy Spirit gave me solace in verses like "Mary pondered these things and kept them in her heart" (Luke 2:19, KJV).

Certainly, I was distressed to think that these people could hold the positions they did and be so moved by the spirit of jealousy. Even when I read about Saul's relentless pursuit of David, I hesitated to draw a correlation to my own situation. I was reluctant to be judgmental and critical of those who opposed me. Instead, I gradually learned to take every accusation and attack to the Lord, to extract the precious from the worthless,[23] or as one friend long ago said, "Chew the meat and spit out the bones."

It wasn't always the first thing I did. But, along the way, there came a time when I heard the Lord

---

23 Jeremiah 15:9

say, "If you keep trying to defend yourself, I can't." What a difference that began to make in how I handled opposition! He avenges, defends, and protects those who call upon Him.[24] It took a long time to learn to trust God in this, and I am not perfect in it yet, but it is ultimately the only thing that brings peace.

Trusting God in little things each day and seeing Him work is essential to our growth. It cannot come from copying what others do. The Apostle Paul's admonition to, "Imitate me, watch my ways, follow my example, just as I, too, always seek to imitate the Anointed One" (1 Corinthians 11:1), like many other things Paul said, can easily be misconstrued. It is dangerous to oversimplify this verse as a justification to preach, "Do what I do."

In fact, thinking this was all a matter of doing what they saw being done, seven sons of a priest named Sceva tried to exorcise a demon from a man. The demon recognized the name of Jesus, and the name of Paul, but not these men. The possessed man attacked them, stripping them and beating them badly.[25]

We must be allowed time to grow in our faith. Jesus was with His disciples for three years, showing

---

24 Luke 18:8
25 Acts 19:14, ff.

them the ways of the Father, telling them the things the Father had said, and giving them power to command demons. Yet, until they received the fullness of the Holy Spirit on the day of Pentecost, they were in a period of waiting.

It has been argued that every believer receives the Holy Spirit when he or she accepts Jesus the Anointed as the sacrifice for his or her sins, entering into relationship with God through faith in Him. It has been argued that this is a different experience from being filled with that same Spirit as on the day of Pentecost. However, neither of these is the same as being led by the Spirit of God.

Whatever God has called us to do as individuals will not be accomplished apart from our cooperation with His Spirit working within us and leading us. This is what Jesus was saying to His followers in John 15. He is the true vine, and they are the branches through which He wants to work. Apart from His life flowing through us, we accomplish nothing, whether we think it's something or not. In spite of all they have done to serve Him, many will be surprised to hear the Lord tell them that He never knew them.[26]

We can debate and argue and strive with one another over what we think is right, but in the end,

---

26 Matthew 7:23

only one thing will matter. Did we know Him intimately enough to do what He told us to do? Did we even hear His voice?

It saddens me to recall the times when God was speaking to me and I chose to listen to church leaders because I thought they knew better, or worse, because I wanted to be accepted so I could receive the praise or recognition I had always yearned for. Yet, because of my determined desire to know Him, and because of His inscrutable wisdom, God, my Father, did not use anyone to provide such acceptance and recognition. Instead, He used all that I went through, causing it all to work together for good,[27] to train me and strengthen me to stand on my own, confident that, come what may, He was leading me.

Likewise, it saddens me to hear so many believers say they don't hear God's voice, when Jesus said we are able to. There is no doubt that the early believers did. What is it that keeps us from hearing it for ourselves in our time?

As already stated, it could be that we need to separate ourselves from the noise. It could be that we don't trust that we really are hearing Him. It could be that the voice of God is speaking something that goes against what we have always thought to be true about Him. Or, we may feel that "all those people can't be

---

27 Romans 8:28

wrong." This can be especially difficult. He may be calling us to leave a group of people we love. We may have heard for countless years that a particular scripture means a particular thing and now we see it in a different way. It could cost us our friends, or our fame, or even "our" ministry.

Yes, it could, or we could end up being the one through whom God speaks and works and wants to reveal Himself to the world. We will never know until we begin to listen, first of all, believing that we can hear Him. It may mean shutting ourselves off from the crowd or from the distractions of our age, but it is vital that we hear Him.

It becomes even more critical when we begin to speak out publicly. This is not just for our personal welfare, but because of the impact our words have on others, especially those who look up to us as being more mature. God's Word is quite clear about what will happen to those who cause His little ones to stumble and fall away.[28]

Jesus was not only speaking about little children here, although the verse can certainly be interpreted that way. He was speaking of those who have just begun their journey of faith in Him, who are tender and eager to please. In either case, the assurance that God is speaking to us must be firmly

28 Mark 9:42, Matthew 18:6, Luke 17:2

established within us. Moreover, before we speak what He is saying to others, we must be willing to stake our lives on it.

12

GOD'S WORD – GOD'S WAY

God's Word

To know God's Word in this age, all that is required is desire. The number of translations and methods for hearing and or reading the Word of God has increased steadily over the last several decades.

Regrettably, many still argue for the use of one particular version, The King James Bible, which was translated in 1611, as the authoritative Word of God. As a result, the majority of those who are subjected to this doctrine don't understand God's Word at all. It's as if they think God's Word is so holy we aren't supposed to understand it. If that is true, how can we hope to do it?

Before the reformers translated the King James Bible, the great Roman Catholic church denied the ability to interpret scripture to everyone but the priesthood. They continued to do so until the middle of the twentieth century. Denying literacy on any level to any group of people is the primary tactic used by oppressive governments to keep people in bondage.

Furthermore, just as newborn babes desire milk, new believers desire the Word of God. If they are fed something else, they do not grow properly. They may learn to mistrust anything that sounds different than what they are accustomed to hearing, having been taught, either implicitly or explicitly, that they can't trust anything else to be true. They certainly can't trust themselves, so even if the Spirit of God is nudging them in a different direction, they will resist it. This is the reason many cults exist. It is also why so many denominations exist.

Nothing can take the place of the knowledge we gain when we encounter the Word of God with the Holy Spirit of God teaching us and guiding us into the truth for ourselves. Accordingly, the ultimate goal of every teacher should be to facilitate life-long learning, rather than to create a dependence on the teacher. Likewise, the objective of every true teacher of God's Word, every pastor, evangelist, prophet, and apostle, should be maturing the believers in the knowledge of God and equipping them to discern and live in the power of God's Spirit for themselves. If it is anything else, it is "another gospel."[29]

---

29 Galatians 1:8

God's Way

Although it is very easy to become comfortable in our own corners with our own dearly held beliefs, favorite hymns, songs and Bible verses, we run the risk of having a very limited view of God's plan. It therefore becomes easier to follow rules and rituals than to follow the leading of the Spirit of God. Unfortunately, the rules and rituals do not give us His life, and it is His life, in abundance, that Jesus died to give us.

In all of his epistles, Paul expresses his concerns that the converts would not learn and grow into mature believers. For the Galatians, he is concerned about their tendency of falling back under the Jewish laws. He writes, "My dear children, I feel the pains of birth upon me again, and I will continue in labor for you until the Anointed One is formed completely in you" (Galatians 4:19).

While the debate continues over who these Galatians were, what was happening in their midst is fairly obvious. They had been thrown into confusion by leaders who were pressuring them to add Old Covenant laws to their faith, so they would be more "acceptable." More specifically, these legalists wanted the new believers in Jesus to be physically circumcised as they had been.

Paul was beside himself. He stated that if they conformed to this Old Covenant rite, they should also conform to all the other laws. Following that to its logical conclusion, they would then nullify the covenant Jesus had shed His blood to initiate. Instead, Paul urges them to be led by the Spirit of God and to stop the "vicious gnawing on one another" (Galatians 5:14).

In Corinth, Paul grappled with the issue of strife and fighting among believers, telling them they needed to be fed spiritual milk, because they were still living in the flesh, not ready to digest complex spiritual food. He knew this because, they were fighting with one another, comparing themselves to each other and becoming consumed with jealousy. "You are living in the flesh, no different from the rest who live by the standards of this rebellious and broken world," he stated (I Corinthians 3:2-3).

It should be clear to us that the New Covenant Jesus gave us is not like the old one. It does not depend on keeping outward laws of conduct or tradition with hearts that remain unchanged. It does not even depend on anything we are humanly capable of doing. It depends on one thing only, and this one thing is given to every person who has ever lived: it is the gift of faith.

This priceless truth has almost been lost in translation. As with the Corinthians, one of Paul's focuses with the Romans was how they treated each other. The Aramaic Bible in Plain English translates the Romans 12:3 as follows:

> *I say to all of you by the grace that is given to me, that you should not have self-esteem beyond what is necessary to have self-esteem, but you should have self-esteem and modesty as God distributes faith to every person by a measure.*

Whereas other translations imply that we should compare ourselves to others by the measure of faith we have received, this translation comes the closest to making sense of this statement. If we substitute the word "because" for the word "as" in the last portion of the statement, the concept becomes even more clear - you should have self-esteem and modesty because God distributes faith to every person by a measure.

These examples emphasize our need for the Holy Spirit Himself to interpret His Word, so that it fits appropriately, not with our doctrine, but with His own nature as it is revealed in the comprehensive plan and purpose of God[30].

Jesus told His followers that the seed, the Word of God, was being sown on everyone. The sower scattered it. He didn't plant it. Where it landed was the determiner of its success. Understanding this parable, of seed falling on rocks, among thorns, and in various types of soil, as said before, is the key to understanding all the other parables.

When Jesus gasped, "It is finished," He proclaimed an end to the work of the law. The veil that covered the Holy of Holies where the presence of God existed under the Old Covenant was torn in two. He proceeded to free the captives of the law in hell and ascend to the right hand of God the Father in heaven. From there, at the throne of Grace, He sent His Holy Spirit to each believer to guide them into truth and to collectively accomplish even greater things, in number, than He had done.

His expectation of us is that we believe He has done this. The only thing God is pleased with is our faith and without faith, there is nothing we can do to please Him.[31]

---

30 Acts 20:27
31 Hebrews 11:6

Our Choice

God has invested this gift of faith, this seed, in each one of us, whether we understand it or not. We can either allow it to grow or to remain dormant. We can allow it full expression to bring forth its fruit in abundance, or we can allow it to be choked and fruitless. It is truly our choice, and He does not make that choice for us. He simply allows us to choose.

No matter what we believe about the times and seasons of His coming, we can certainly agree that we are over 2000 years closer to that time than the original audience was. In Matthew's gospel, chapter 25, there are two parables of Jesus that refer to the kingdom of God and to the end time.

Both parables describe a variety of responses to a particular important event: the return of the Master. In the first parable, He is represented as the bridegroom. While the bridegroom delays His coming, ten virgins wait to attend the wedding feast. When modern Christians hear "bridegroom and bride," we usually associate the bride with the Church and the bridegroom with Jesus. But to the original audience, the bride and groom were still a great mystery. The marriage supper of the lamb is part of the Revelation to John that occurred on the isle of Patmos in AD 95. So, it seems more appropriate to interpret these words as they were presented to the original audience.

What we know is that all the virgins were awaiting the bridegroom's arrival. Customarily, this was at night, so the attendants would go out to meet him with their lanterns lighting the way. We are told that five of them were wise. They were prepared; they had oil for their lamps and a spare supply.

We know that all the attendants fell asleep waiting, but the wise ones were ready at a moment's notice because they had taken their responsibility seriously. They had continued to give freely from what they had received and were continually supplied with more. They had extra oil … an overflow. They kept their wicks trimmed so they would burn brightly. They left nothing undone. In other words, they had never stopped being ready for the bridegroom's return.

The other five attendants had interpreted the long delay in the bridegroom's arrival as an opportunity to serve themselves. They did not consider a personal relationship to God and His commandments to be their responsibility. They knew where they could go to get a little oil now and then, but they didn't maintain their own supply, because it wasn't important to them do so. When the bridegroom came, these foolish attendants knew who

He was, but they were unable to join the procession because they did not have their own oil.

Most studies of biblical symbolism tell us that oil signifies the Holy Spirit, or the anointing of God. This doesn't mean these foolish ones weren't filled with the Holy Spirit at some point, but they did not do what was necessary to be continually filled with the Holy Spirit, following His leading and yielding their vessels to Him as living sacrifices.

Although the wise had evidently given freely of their supply in the past, even to the foolish, they understood that this time what they possessed could not be shared. The record does not explain why. Perhaps they recognized the time was so short, they would need every ounce of what they had to fulfill their mission. They knew there was no time left.

This was the event the wise had been training for, waiting for, ready for. The time of teaching others to know Him was over.

They should all have known Him intimately by now. As Jeremiah prophesied, "They will not need to teach their neighbors, nor will they need to teach their relatives, saying, 'You should know the LORD.' For everyone, from the least to the greatest, will know me already" (31:34). The wise virgin attendants had not neglected their responsibility, but their mission now was to escort the bridegroom to the feast, while the others stayed in the darkness.

God did not withhold anything from the foolish five. It was what they chose to believe that kept them from experiencing what the others had prepared for. They didn't believe they needed to prepare themselves. They considered it to be someone else's job. In the end, they heard the words, "I never knew you." The Lord didn't know them because they had not faithfully attended to their own relationship with Him.

The ten virgin attendants are an allegory of the Church. Hence, it is not only possible, but probable that 50% of the church will not be ready to meet Jesus for the wedding supper.

The second parable in Matthew 25 about the kingdom of heaven tells us of the landowner who leaves three different servants with investments, each according to his (or her) ability. Once again, we see that a choice was made. It was a simple, incremental choice based on what they believed about the landowner.

To one servant, the landowner gave five portions, to another three, and to the last one he gave one portion.

This landowner already knew who was most likely to make the best investment. Two of the servants doubled their assets, skillfully and attentively increasing them with their own labor.

The third servant decided the safest thing to do was to bury his portion in a hole. His perception of the landowner was that he was stingy, unjust, and demanding. This point of view was so repulsive to the landowner that he ordered the servant bound and thrown into the darkness. We need to ask ourselves why his perception of the landowner was so different.

In spite of the specific details and differences of these two parables, they both highlight a single, central truth: It was what those waiting for the Master's return believed about Him that determined both the action they took and the outcome they ultimately received.

Both parables about the kingdom of Heaven speak to our life under the New Covenant, the covenant of faith in Jesus the Anointed One, Christ. What do we really believe about Him?

Some who call themselves His people actually believe He is harsh and unjust. They believe it is safer to not do anything with what He has entrusted to them, their giftings, their abilities, so they do their best to give Him what they owe Him and let it go at that.

Others who are called His people believe that His promises are conditional and that the conditions depend on His will and something they do, but they aren't really sure what that may be. They might get to eat dessert if they eat all their spinach, but they aren't sure about that either, because they don't really understand or believe what God will do.

Finally, there are some of His people who believe that God wants to display His goodness to them and to receive, in return, the fullness of the earth through them. They believe in the gift of faith, the seed He has placed within them. They put their faith into operation and do great things for His glory, believing they will receive all the blessings of the kingdom of His grace.

What is the difference between them? It is what they believe about God. He is the very same Master, but He is perceived differently by each of them, based on what they choose to believe about Him. And this belief about Him determines whether they will even obey Him, just as in the parable. The Master gave each of the servants a portion of His wealth and instructed them, "trade with this until I return." Yet, because of what he believed, one of them didn't even make an attempt to obey.

Throughout all the covenants, those who did not receive what God promised were the ones who did not combine His promises with faith. They didn't actually operate in faith, so the promises did them no good.[32]

When the spies of Israel were sent into the Promised Land to bring back a report, they failed to consider all the good things God had done. He had provided for them over and over after bringing them out of slavery in Egypt. Yet, instead of seeing that God was certainly able to do what He promised, to defeat the inhabitants of the land He had promised to give them, they chose to look at their own strength and inability.

They spread discouraging rumors throughout the camp. They paid for it with their lives. The people who believed the reports were prevented from going in and receiving the promises. In fact, only two of the entire nation were able to enter the land, and it was forty years later, after all the offenders had died in the wilderness.[33]

In this New Covenant, all things pertaining to life and godliness have already been invested in us, and the power to experience these blessings depends entirely upon what we believe about God, because that alone determines what we do with what we have been given. We must understand that we have taken a Blood Covenant Oath, paid for with the earth-life

---

32 Hebrews 4:2
33 Numbers 14:20-23

of Jesus. Not only is His life now our life, but our individual lives are His. It is therefore, absolutely essential that we are able to hear His Spirit, His Counsel, or as discussed earlier, His Voice, and that we each do what He is instructing us to do. Our reasonable, essential response is to offer ourselves and our lives to God and His will, our faith bringing Him pleasure. This is real worship. [34]

34 Romans 12:1

13

CAFETERIA COVENANT
The Covenant of Choice

We are stepping through a narrow door into a marvelous dispensation of goodness and blessing, healing, prosperity, and victory. We can choose from among this glorious cafeteria of blessings as we abide in Him. This is what it is to really believe Jesus' words in John 15, that we can ask what we will and it will be done for us because we abide in Him and His Word abides in us. Nothing truly good is provided by any other means.

If this is true, what prevents us from truly abiding and believing? Moreover, what keeps the church from living in the power Jesus sent them and told them to employ?

I believe the answer is found in Jesus' prayer for His followers (John 17):

May they be one even as We are one... I have given them Your word; and the world has despised them because they are not products of the world, in the same way that I am not a product of the corrupt world order...

Immerse them in the truth, the truth Your voice speaks. In the same way You sent Me into this world, I am sending them.

It is entirely for their benefit that I have set Myself apart so that they may be set apart by truth. I am not asking solely for their benefit; this prayer is also for all the believers who will follow them and hear them speak.

Father, may they all be one as You are in Me and I am in You; may they be in Us, for by this unity the world will believe that You sent Me (John 17:11-21).

Jesus' expressed will in this New Covenant is that the unity of His followers would be so evident that it would cause the world to believe the Father had sent Him. He had taught it to them by example again and again. He had spoken it to them at the last supper, as He washed their feet. And in His final recorded prayer, He had prayed for it to be so. It is not for one specific group or one unique period in history; it is for all time and for all believers.

Why have we not yet seen this unity?

We must first realize that it will not be by our own strength, but by our willingness to receive direction from the Spirit of God. The unity Jesus was speaking to His Father about was His own unity with His Father, God. If we do not have oneness with Him, we will never have it with other believers. That is its source. Each of us must allow His Spirit to change us and make us one with Him and with the Father.

We must begin by putting aside our comfort and convenience and simply make ourselves available to Him. This is our reasonable service of worship, as we are told in Romans 12:1. We must lay aside the arguing, the strife, and the division, recognizing that these things are marks of the immaturity of the church.

Both inside and outside the walls of the church, there are many who feel compelled to argue their own idiosyncratic beliefs. They are in the marketplace, scorning the numerous translations of God's Word, proclaiming them to be heresy because they are not the Authorized King James Version...

They are on social networks, spouting their knowledge and wrangling over the interpretation of words. They respond to blogs that were formed to unite those with common interests, denouncing those who believe that God wants us to prosper and be in health even as our souls prosper...[35]

They are sequestered in churches and private schools, monitoring appropriate attire and hoping to escape the corruption that is in the world...

They are fighting and biting and killing the wounded, and much worse, destroying the faith of young believers...

This is the work of the enemy that has prevailed. This is how he keeps us from maturing into the fullness of the anointing of Christ, the Anointed One.

God has always wanted his people to be in unity. David the Psalmist described this unity as the sweet-smelling oil poured out on the priest's head, flowing like gentle rain from the mountain of God, where God promises his blessing of eternal life.[36] This oil, as in other places, is symbolic of the Holy

---

35 3 John 1:2
36 Psalm 133

Spirit, He who unites us to God the Father and God the Son.

I've even heard: "Some Christians think they can pick and choose what they believe about God, as if His kingdom were some kind of a cafeteria!" Yet, I have come to realize this is exactly as God intended. God will not force us to believe what we have no desire to believe. It is our right to believe what we want and likewise our right to receive according to that belief.

In fact, accepting this fact, our right to choose, may prove to be the very thing that begins to restore the unity for which Jesus prayed. We must respect that right for the sake of the unity of His body.

We cannot deny that right to anyone. Though he was not faithful, the prodigal's son was still a son. He abused the blessings the Father wanted him to experience, but he was still a son. We cannot threaten or try to manipulate or dictate to other believers in the name of Love.

What we can and must do is draw upon God's Love, continue to extend grace, and continue to let living water flow through us to them. We can and must continue praying for God to open eyes and hearts to the truth, and from that heart of love, speak what the Spirit of the Lord directs us to speak, without regard for how we might be treated.

The power to choose is a God-given right and privilege, restored to us as it was in the Garden of Eden through the sacrifice of Jesus the Anointed, Messiah. Our choice continues moment by moment, day by day. It will remain our choice alone that determines whether He lives in us and bears His fruit through us or not. It will never stop being our choice.

His plan is that we become increasingly dependent upon Him as our life source and for the good things of His kingdom, instead of our own ability or the world's ideas of success. In this way, as our mind, will, and emotions are re-formed, we are transformed into His likeness.[37]

I am convinced that if we choose to yield to His life, we will experience Life as we have never known it and perhaps never imagined it could be. Moreover, we will be able to look back on our experiences and realize that we really have been part of something far greater than we could have asked or thought.

---

37 Romans 12:1-2

14

THE LIVING SACRIFICE

When I first came to understand that Jesus died for me, I was so overwhelmed by His Love, I meditated on it daily. I sought His love in my studying and found it woven through both the Old and New Covenants. I realized that it was God's Love that Jesus came to reveal. It was what Jesus told His disciples to do. It was the reason He sacrificed himself to be put to death. He could have called thousands of angels to His rescue.[38] Instead, he chose to give His life in obedience to the plan of God, to redeem us from the bondage of this world and its trappings: the power of sin and death. Love was behind every law God gave in the Old Covenant, and it is the law of the new one.

God's love is uniquely HIS, bestowed on us through His grace and poured into our receptive hearts so that it will continue on its course

---

38 Matthew 26:53

unhindered to accomplish what it was sent forth to do. His love will always be His. It is only ours only by yielding to it.

The purpose of knowledge is different. It is ours to explore, to gain information and understanding, so that the power of Love within us can find its way across any breach and any distance. When we allow knowledge to become our highest aim, it makes us feel good, because knowledge is attained by our own effort.

I once worked at a Christian school where more than 40 different churches were represented across the students and staff. Occasions arose daily to challenge the beliefs of fellow workers and students. Some of my colleagues took the opportunity to do just that. Yet, while there were things I would have liked to say, God did not give me the grace to say them. I did not believe it was what I was there to do.

Although we should certainly stand up for what we believe in in this world, as believers, we must recognize that our mission is to love one another. Love builds up; it does not tear down, either by commission or omission. Knowledge, by contrast, "puffs up." [39]

---

39 1 Corinthians 8:1-13

I have fellowship with Christian friends whose beliefs about how to worship God are quite different from my own. We don't focus on what is different about us. Instead, we appreciate our respective customs and who we are as individuals: different parts of the same body. We marvel at the diversity of expression and receive each other with grace, and focus on what we have in common: our faith in Jesus Christ.

I also have friends who are of different faiths. I extend love and grace to them, believing God is in me and that through me, they may yet come to know the One I know because He is in me.

My mission is to show them what is right by my course of action; it is not to tell them they are wrong. I am not suggesting we should be silent when a fellow believer is heading down a wayward path; I am speaking of those who do not yet believe in Jesus as the Anointed One.

I also have "friends" who have been dead for years, some even for centuries; yet I have fellowship with them through their words, in spirit-to-spirit agreement. Other "friends" are still alive, but I have met them only through the acknowledgement of the same truth. They come from an incredibly diverse array of backgrounds and denominations.

Epilogue

The Council

Over the last few weeks, I have been astounded to repeatedly encounter the confirmation of the things I have endeavored to express in this book. Earlier this week in my devotions, I read some of these thoughts expressed by two contemporary, world- renowned, and highly respected author-teachers. This morning, I turned the page in my Bible to the devotion I marked a year ago; a year had passed since the revelation of the Cafeteria Covenant I wrote about in my preface to this work.

I have contemplated using the exact words of this council of wise and Godly influences by weaving them together into a unified "voice," with footnotes to acknowledge each of them, respectively. But as more and more of them began to "speak," I realized that the task of getting permissions from each of them could take months, if it ever was accomplished.

Furthermore, while I call them my "friends," they, in fact, don't know me and their publishers may not wish to risk involvement in a little book from a virtually unknown author. So, with the exception of those whose works are now public domain, I will not mention their names, nor will I quote from their works.

The message is not their own, nor is it mine, and it is not new. Yet, it is apparently as controversial today as it was in the early Church.

When I sat down to write this evening (June 2012), the words, "See how these Christians love each other," came to mind. I discovered the words are attributed to an early defender of the faith named Tertullian, who wrote things that flew in the face of what had already become, by the spring of AD 197, an organized religion of bishops.

Among other things, he asserted that the Church represented the people of the Holy Spirit. As I researched him briefly on the Internet, I discovered more. Tertullian wrote the following:

> But it is mainly the deeds of a love so noble that lead many to put a brand upon us. See, they say, how they love one another, for they themselves are animated by mutual hatred. See, they say about us, how they are ready even to die for one another, for they themselves would sooner kill.

These believers stood out from the rest of the world because of a profound difference in how they treated one another. It was not what they wore or did not wear, nor was it what they said or did not say; it was how they treated one another in the daily course of their lives that set them apart from others. At the same time, the earliest believers in Jesus were able to turn the world upside down.[40]

The power of God was shown in their lives, confirming the Word of

the Lord, "with signs following."[41] This love and unity and the power of God that accompanied it were the identity of the early Church. This was not an identity that was achieved by a campaign for boldness to witness nor increased contempt of the world. It was not accomplished by teaching about self-esteem or by adhering to ritual or tradition. It was the natural product of something we seem to have lost sight of today. Andrew Murray (1828-1917) expressed it this way:

> Therefore, let us put on a heart of compassion, kindness, humility, meekness, long-suffering; and let us prove our Christlikeness, not only in our zeal for saving the lost, but before all in our

---

40 Acts 17:1-9
41 Mark 16:20

intercourse with the brethren, forbearing and forgiving one another, even as the Lord forgave us.

Fellow Christians, do let us study the Bible portrait of the humble man. And let us ask our brethren, and ask the world, whether they recognize in us the likeness to the original. Let us be content with nothing less than taking each of these texts as the promise of what God will work in us, as the revelation in words of what the Spirit of Jesus will give as a birth within us. And let each failure and shortcoming simply urge us to turn humbly and meekly to the meek and lowly Lamb of God, in the assurance that where He is enthroned in the heart, His humility and gentleness will be one of the streams of living water that flow from within us.[42]

Among Christians of today, even the concept of being like Jesus is in dispute. Being humble is defined by some as being weak, by others as being poor; still others define it as self-denigration. It is none of these things. True Christ-like humility is yield-ed-ness to the Spirit of God who desires to live within us and flow out to others.

---

42 *Humility in the Daily Life*, Andrew Murray, nd

If we consider ourselves redeemed by the blood Jesus shed, He is our brother, the first-born of many. He was led in all things by the Spirit of God within Him and was our model for how to live.

Jesus told His followers that streams of living water would flow from those who believe. He didn't speak of developing evangelism programs or adapting worship services to appeal to the masses. He did not speak of self-realization or self-preservation. Furthermore, it is not humility to think of ourselves as worthless, as the dirt under the toenail of the body of Christ, or as just poor old sinners saved by grace. In fact, such thinking and the words uttered in defense of it are an insult to His redemptive work. How can we call the denial of His work in us humility? How can we say He is not faithful to His promises when He says He is? Do we really think this is pleasing to God?

Andrew Murray expressed the secret of true Christianity as, "The daily, unceasing faith in what Jesus will work in us each moment of our life. When this faith is not exercised and sought after, the Christian life becomes feeble. Nothing grieves the Holy Spirit as much as the unbelief which prevents Jesus from showing His power to deliver men from the power of sin and the world."[43]

---

43 Ibid

Unfortunately, the very issue of faith itself has become the source of a great schism among believers. We are like sheep without a shepherd instead of sheep of the great shepherd all hearing His voice. And so, division occurs more rapidly than multiplication.

I believe this division over faith is one of the greatest hindrances to the growth of the body of the Anointed (Christ) into its fullness and power in the world today. As an example, consider the widespread derogatory term, "Name it and Claim it Bunch," usually accompanied by accounts of extravagant abuse and mockery. As a result of this slander, the whole revelation of the life of faith, all the New Testament teaching on the keys of the Kingdom of God, and how we are to really live in this world are thoughtlessly discarded, along with the quite biblical concept of the power of the tongue.

Is it any wonder the world looks on and says, if God is in control, why are children being abused and murdered, why are millions starving and dying of diseases that have cures? If God is in control, what kind of a God is He/She?

For that matter, if God is in control, why aren't Christians, at the very least, under control of their own emotions, words, and lives?

I do not claim to have all the answers or solutions about why some are not healed. I can only refer to what the Word of God says, as I have done many times through this book, and appeal to you, the reader, to consider that we have a covenant with God that provides every promise He has made to man.[44] If we are not willing to believe that, we may not really be living by faith.

As a new convert, before I ever heard of "faith" teaching, I read James 3:2-6. In it, the biological half-brother of Jesus writes:

> *If a person never speaks hurtful words or shouts in anger or profanity, then he has achieved perfection. The one who can control his tongue can also control the rest of his body. It's like when we place a metal bit into a horse's mouth to ride it; we can control its entire body with the slightest movement of our hands. Have you ever seen a massive ship sailing effortlessly across the water? Despite its immense size and the fact that it is propelled by mighty winds, a small rudder directs the ship in any direction the pilot chooses. It's just the same with our tongues! It's a small muscle, capable of marvelous undertakings.*

---

44 2 Corinthians 1:20

James continues by stating that it is not within the power of humankind to control the tongue. But is it not within God's power? In Mark's account of Jesus' words (11:23-26), we read:

> *Trust in God. If you do, honestly, you can say to this mountain, "Mountain, uproot yourself and throw yourself into the sea." If you don't doubt, but trust that what you say will take place, then it will happen. So listen to what I'm saying: Whatever you pray for or ask from God, believe that you'll receive it and you will. When you pray, if you remember anyone who has wronged you, forgive him so that God above can also forgive you. [If you don't forgive others, don't expect God's forgiveness.]*

I was still a relatively young believer when I stood in an assembly of faith-teaching followers and tried to share a message about the love of God with them. God had given me a song based on the following verses from 1 Thessalonians 3:12-13:

> *...and may the Lord cause you to increase and abound in love for one another, and for all people, just as we also do for you; so that He may establish*

your hearts without blame in holiness before our
God and Father at the coming of our Lord Jesus
with all His saints.

It seemed clear to me that no matter what else we have done, to be found without blame and holy at His coming, we must increase and abound in the work of loving one another.

Unfortunately, the leaders of this particular group neither had this revelation, nor the grace to receive it. "Singers aren't teachers," the appointed pastor said as he confronted me and asked me to sit down. Quoting from the King James Bible, the elders argued later, "Faith worketh by love."

Even I could see that in spite of their titles and my lack thereof, they were applying a portion of a verse out of context to reinforce their own position. Galatians 5:6 is the second part of an argument Paul was making against being subject to the rituals of the law. Even in the King James Bible, the meaning should be clear to anyone who wants to understand:

"For in Jesus Christ neither circumcision availeth anything, nor uncircumcision; but faith which worketh by love."

I was shocked that they couldn't see it. But now, having taught several hundred high school

English students, I realize not everyone fully understands how to interpret modern English, let alone 17th century English.

In the second part of the sentence, there is no verb. The verb is "availeth" from the first part of the sentence, and in modern English, it means to be of use or advantage.

With this understanding, we can translate the verse as follows: "For in Jesus Christ neither circumcision is of use or advantage, nor is uncircumcision of use or advantage; but faith which worketh by love is of use or advantage.

Faith that is motivated and working by love is of use and advantage. But faith alone does not encompass love. Perhaps this is why Paul was compelled to write the treatise on God's love in 1 Corinthians 13:

> *If I [can] speak in the tongues of men and [even] of angels, but have not love (that reasoning, intentional, spiritual devotion such as is inspired by God's love for and in us), I am only a noisy gong or a clanging cymbal.*
>
> *2 And if I have prophetic powers (the gift of interpreting the divine will and purpose), and understand all the secret truths and mysteries and possess all knowledge, and if I have [sufficient] faith so that I can remove mountains,*

but have not love (God's love in me) I am nothing (a useless nobody).

3 Even if I dole out all that I have [to the poor in providing] food, and if I surrender my body to be burned or in order that I may glory, but have not love (God's love in me), I gain nothing.

4 Love endures long and is patient and kind; love never is envious nor boils over with jealousy, is not boastful or vainglorious, does not display itself haughtily.

5 It is not conceited (arrogant and inflated with pride); it is not rude (unmannerly) and does not act unbecomingly. Love (God's love in us) does not insist on its own rights or its own way, for it is not self-seeking; it is not touchy or fretful or resentful; it takes no account of the evil done to it [it pays no attention to a suffered wrong].

6 It does not rejoice at injustice and unrighteousness, but rejoices when right and truth prevail …

13 And so faith, hope, love abide [faith— conviction and belief respecting man's relation to God and divine things; hope—joyful and confident expectation of eternal salvation; love— true affection for God and man, growing out of God's love for and in us], these three; but the greatest of these is love. (Amplified Bible).

The power to live the way God wants us to live was extended to us when we first entered our covenant of faith in Jesus, the Anointed. This does not mean we can expect to be perfect instantly or to be Christ-like by our own effort; it means that the work of faith within us has begun. Only begun. Our roots grow deeper as we employ this faith in love for God and for one another. We live for, and because of, His promises, believing in spite of seeing and feeling.

Those who allow His Spirit to work through them are the great heroes of faith. They have developed a relationship to the Father through the Son and are able to trust Him more each day. They consider their own lives expendable so that His life can have expression. Their words are empowered by love for God, His Word, His promises, and the fellow inhabitants of His creation. They are partners in His work on the earth. This is what it means to die to self, to offer ourselves as living sacrifices to His will.

In all of God's covenants, He issues the invitation to choose. To become part of His great body on the earth is a choice and encompassed in this choice are the abundant blessings of life, peace, health, and prosperity. Blessings are the effects of His life; they are not the life itself.

My prayer for you, reader, is that you will be willing to lay aside your personal opinions and beliefs long enough to see that you are meant to be part of something that goes beyond the walls of any present-day church, and beyond your personal likes, dislikes and opinions. God wants to display His goodness in the earth in a powerful, wonderfully alive way. His abundant and rich cafeteria full of blessings is eternally open, filled with "great and valuable promises," so that we may "share in the divine nature,"[45] so that the world will come to know Jesus, because we are one with Him and He lives in us.

Only by knowing the truth can the real Church be free to rise up, in its full power. The desperate world needs to see and experience the genuine, uncontrived power of God. It begins with what we really believe about God and extends to what we believe about each other. What will be your choice?

---

45 2 Peter 1:4

Livingwell Seed Co. is dedicated to the edification of the Body of Christ. It is a place to find encouragement to LIVE WELL in this world, through the revelation of God's Word, the ministry of spiritual song, and the beauty that surrounds us.

Please visit www.LivwellSeedCo.com for more information or to connect with us.